PUFFIN BOOKS

The Pain-in-the

At last, a joke bo
groan. Not since
Vampire's Victim has there been such a ghastly (or
should I say ghostly) book. With jokes about
every 'orrible creature you could possibly imagine
– from vampires to werewolves, from skeletons to
bats, from witches to ghouls – there's something
here to keep you and your friends howling for
years and years!

Martyn Forrester has been a teacher (could this
be where he heard all these jokes?), advertising
copy-writer and journalist. He lives in London
with his three children.

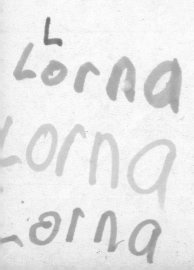

The Pain-in-the-Neck Joke Book

Alison Irwin

Martyn Forrester

Illustrated by Doffy Weir

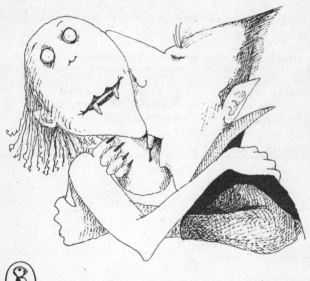

PUFFIN BOOKS

PUFFIN BOOKS

Published by the Penguin Group
Penguin Books Ltd, 27 Wrights Lane, London w8 5tz, England
Penguin Books USA Inc., 375 Hudson Street, New York, New York 10014, USA
Penguin Books Australia Ltd, Ringwood, Victoria, Australia
Penguin Books Canada Ltd, 10 Alcorn Avenue, Toronto, Ontario, Canada m3v 3b2
Penguin Books (NZ) Ltd, 182–190 Wairau Road, Auckland 10, New Zealand

Penguin Books Ltd, Registered Offices: Harmondsworth, Middlesex, England

First published 1991
10 9 8 7 6 5 4 3 2 1

Printed in England by Clays Ltd, St Ives plc
Filmset in Monophoto Plantin

In this 'orrible book are:

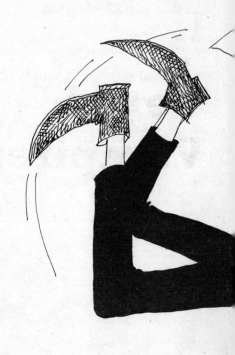

1.

Vexed Vampires

Why do some vampires eat raw meat?
Because they don't know how to cook.

What happens to vampires when it rains?
They get wet.

What is ugly and scary and has eight
   wheels?
A vampire on roller-skates.

VAMPIRE TO SHOPKEEPER: How much are
   your black candles?
SHOPKEEPER: *A pound each.*
VAMPIRE: That's candlous!

How can you tell if a vampire has been at
   your tomato juice?
By the teeth-marks on the lid.

What do you call a vampire with a car on
   his head?
Jack.

Who did Dracula marry?
His ghoul-friend.

What's the name of Dracula's cook?
Fangy Craddock.

What do you call the spot in the middle
of a graveyard?
The dead centre.

1ST VAMPIRE: You should keep control of your little boy. He just bit me on the ankle.

2ND VAMPIRE: *That's only because he couldn't reach your neck.*

1ST VAMPIRE: Shall I buy black or white candles?

2ND VAMPIRE: *Which burn longer?*

1ST VAMPIRE: Neither, they both burn shorter.

What is the best way of stopping infection from vampire bites?
Don't bite any vampires!

VAMPIRE: I'd like some new tiles for my bathroom.

ASSISTANT: *But, madam, this is a pet shop.*

VAMPIRE: That's all right – I want reptiles.

What is a vampire's favourite TV programme?
Strange Hill.

What do you get if you cross a vampire with a flea?
Lots of very worried dogs.

If you saw nine vampires outside
Woolworth's in black capes and one
vampire outside Boots in a blood-red
cape, what would that prove?
*That nine out of ten vampires wear black
capes.*

What sort of soup do vampires like?
One with plenty of body in it.

A man was walking behind a hearse with
a big vampire's cat on a lead. Behind
them stretched a long line of mourners.
'What happened?' asked a passer-by.
'The vampire's cat bit my wife, and she
died of fright.' 'Can I borrow it?' the
passer-by asked. The man pointed behind
him. 'Get in the queue,' he said.

Why did Dracula miss lunch?
Because he didn't fancy the stake.

How do vampires know that S is a scary
letter?
Because it makes cream scream.

VAMPIRE BOY: What would I have to give
you to get a little kiss?
VAMPIRE GIRL: *Chloroform.*

What is ugly, scary and very blue?
A vampire holding his breath.

Did you hear about the stupid vampire?
*He thought the great smell of Brut was the
   Incredible Hulk's BO!*

1ST VAMPIRE: I don't think much of your
   sister's neck.
2ND VAMPIRE: *Never mind – eat the
   vegetables instead.*

Did you hear about the vampire that has
   pedestrian eyes?
They look both ways before they cross.

What do you call a vampire who has fallen
    into the sea and can't swim?
Bob.

How do you make a vampire float?
*Take two scoops of ice cream, a glass of
    Coke and add one vampire!*

Did you hear about the vampire who went
    on a crash diet?
He wrecked three cars and a bus.

What do you call a vampire who lies on
    the floor all the time?
Matt.

Did you hear about the vampire who ate
    a sofa and two chairs?
He had a suite tooth.

What do you call a vampire who's black
    and blue all over?
Bruce.

Did you hear about the vampire with five
    legs?
His trousers fit him like a glove.

What is a vampire after it is one-year-old?
A two-year-old vampire.

TEACHER: In the vampire family, there was the mother, the father, the grandmother and the little baby. How many does that make?

PUPIL: *Three – and one to carry.*

What's a vampire's worst enemy?
Fang decay.

What do you call a vampire who gets up
  your nose?
Vic.

Mrs Vampire has such an ugly baby she
  doesn't push the pram – she pulls it.

MRS VAMPIRE: Will you love me when
  I'm old and ugly?
MR VAMPIRE: *Darling, of course I do.*

BOY VAMPIRE: What would you like for
  your birthday, sis?
GIRL VAMPIRE: *I'd love a frock to match
  the colour of my eyes.*
BOY VAMPIRE: All right, but where am I
  going to get a bloodshot dress?

A very posh man was walking around an
  art gallery when he stopped by one
  particular exhibit. 'I suppose this
  picture of a hideous vampire is what
  you call modern art,' he said very
  pompously. 'No, sir,' replied the
  assistant, 'that's what we call a
  mirror.'

1ST HUMAN BOY: Why do you keep throwing bunches of garlic out of the window?

2ND HUMAN BOY: *To keep the vampires away.*

1ST HUMAN BOY: But there are no vampires aound here.

2ND HUMAN BOY: *Jolly effective, isn't it?*

How do you know when you're in bed with a vampire?
Because he's got a big V on his pyjamas.

When should you feed vampire's milk to a baby?
When it's a baby vampire.

What do you get if you cross King Kong with a vampire's bat?
A monster that climbs up the Empire State Building and catches planes with its tongue.

PATIENT: Doctor, doctor, you've got to help me – I keep dreaming of bats, creepy-crawlies, demons, ghosts, monsters, vampires, werewolves and yetis . . .

DOCTOR: *How very interesting! Do you always dream in alphabetical order?*

Monster graffiti: GET THE VAMPIRE
BEFORE IT GETS AARRGGH!

What do you call a vampire moving
through the leaves at midnight?
Russell.

Which old song did Dracula hate?
'*Peg O' My Heart.*'

'I bet I can get you to forget about the
vampire.'
'*What vampire?*'
'See, you've forgotten already.'

Could you kill a vampire just by throwing
   eggs at him?
Of course – he'd be eggs-terminated.

1ST VAMPIRE: I feel half-dead.
2ND VAMPIRE: *We'll arrange for you to be
   buried up to your waist.*

'Doctor, doctor, you must help me!'
'What's the problem?'
'Every night I dream there are thousands
   of vampires under my bed. What on
   earth can I do?'
'Saw the legs off your bed.'

When the picture of the vampire's
   grandfather crashed to the floor in the
   middle of the night, what did it mean?
That the nail had come out of the wall.

What is the best way to see a vampire?
On television.

What did the vampire write on his
   Christmas cards?
Best vicious of the season.

If a boxer was knocked out by Dracula,
   what would he be?
Out for the Count.

What's pink, has a curly tail and drinks
  blood?
A hampire.

1ST VAMPIRE: I'm going to a party tonight.
2ND VAMPIRE: *Oh, are you?*
1ST VAMPIRE: Yes, I must go to the
  graveyard and dig out a few old friends.

What did the vampire say when he saw
  the neck of the sleeping man?
'*Ah, breakfast in bed!*'

How does a vampire get through life with
   only one fang?
He has to grin and bare it.

What is Dracula's favourite pudding?
Leeches and scream.

What is a vampire's favourite fruit?
Blood oranges.

What is a vampire's second favourite
   fruit?
Neck-tarines.

What do you get if you cross a vampire
   with a mummy?
A flying bandage.

What do you get if you cross a vampire
   with a rose?
*A flower that goes for your throat when you
   sniff it.*

Did you hear about the doctor who
   crossed a parrot with a vampire?
*It bit his neck, sucked his blood and said,
   'Who's a pretty boy then?'*

Why did the vampire go to the
   psychiatrist?
Because she thought everybody loved her.

What is a vampire's favourite slogan?
Please Give Blood Generously.

Did you hear about the vampire who fell
   into a barrel of beer?
He came to a bitter end.

What's the difference between a musician
and a dead vampire?
One composes and the other decomposes.

What do you get if you cross an owl with
a vampire?
A bird that's ugly but doesn't give a hoot.

What did the vampire say to his
girlfriend?
'After the film, do you fancy a bite?'

Who is the fastest vampire in the world?
Count Dragula.

Why did the vampire's girlfriend break up
with him?
*Because he had such a powerful crush on
her.*

What is a vampire's favourite TV
programme?
Horror-nation Street.

FRIEND TO VAMPIRE MOTHER: Goodness,
hasn't your little girl grown!
VAMPIRE MOTHER: *Yes, she's certainly
gruesome!*

Why are vampires sometimes called
   simple-minded?
Because they're known to be suckers.

What kind of boats do vampires like?
Blood vessels.

Why did the vampire visit Russell Grant?
Because he wanted to see his horrorscope.

What is it called when a vampire gets a
   lot of letters from his admirers?
Fang mail.

What is the best way to speak to a
   vampire?
From a long distance.

What does a polite vampire say?
'Fang you very much.'

What do you call a friendly and handsome
   vampire?
A failure.

Did you hear about the two blood cells?
They loved in vein.

DRACULA: We're going on holiday
  tomorrow.
DRACULA'S WIFE: *Remind me to cancel our
  daily pint of blood.*

What is Dracula's favourite breakfast?
Readyneck.

What's it called when a vampire kisses you
  good-night?
Necking.

Where does Dracula keep his money?
In a blood bank.

What do you get if you cross a midget
with Dracula?
*A vampire that sucks blood from your
kneecaps.*

Where does Dracula get all his jokes?
From his cryptwriter.

Where do vampire ladies have their hair
done?
At the ugly parlour.

YOUNG VAMPIRE: Mummy, Mummy,
what's a vampire?
MUMMY VAMPIRE: *Shut up and drink
your soup before it clots.*

Did you hear about the girl vampire who
wasn't pretty and wasn't ugly?
She was pretty ugly.

What is bright red and dumb?
A blood clot.

Count Dracula has denied that he is to
marry Princess Vampire.
They're just going to remain good fiends.

Why did the vampire actress turn down
   so many film offers?
*She was waiting for a part that she could
   get her teeth into.*

What does a vampire take for a bad cold?
Coffin drops.

Why does Dracula live in a coffin?
Because the rent is low.

What do you think of horror films?
Fangtastic!

What's a vampire's favourite tourist spot?
The Vampire State Building.

What do vampires do every night at eleven
o'clock?
Take a coffin break.

What happens when vampires hold beauty
contests?
Nobody wins.

Why are vampire families close?
Because blood is thicker than water.

When he's out driving, where does
Dracula like to stop and eat?
The Happy Biter.

What did the vampire say when he refused
his dinner?
'Don't worry, I'll have a bite later.'

Where do vampires go fishing?
In the blood stream.

How do vampires like their food
   prepared?
Bite-sized portions.

What do you call a vampire wearing
   ear-muffs?
Anything you like – he can't hear you.

What do you call a short vampire?
A pain in the knee.

What is a vampire's favourite hobby?
In-grave-ing.

What's the difference between a vampire
with toothache and a rainstorm?
*One roars with pain and the other pours
with rain.*

What is Dracula's favourite breed of dog?
The bloodhound.

What is red, sweet and bites people in the
neck?
A jampire.

Who is a vampire likely to fall in love
with?
The girl necks door.

What relation is Dracula to
Frankenstein?
They're blood brothers.

What do you call a duck with fangs?
Count Quackula.

Why did Dracula go to Olympia?
To see the Hearse of the Year Show.

What do you call an old and foolish
    vampire?
A silly old sucker.

Why is Dracula a good person to take out
    to dinner?
Because he eats necks to nothing.

What is Dracula's favourite drink?
A Bloody Mary.

What is Dracula's motto?
The Morgue the Merrier.

Why did the vampire fly over the
 mountain?
Because he couldn't fly under it.

BOOOOKS FROM THE
 VAMPIRE'S LIBRARY:

The Vampire's Victim by E. Drew Blood
Chased by a Werewolf by Claude Bottom
The Omen by B. Warned
Foaming at the Mouth by Dee Monic
Monster From Another Planet by A. Lee-
 En
I Saw a Witch by Denise R. Knockin
In the Witch's Cauldron by Mandy
 Ceased
Boo! by Terry Fie
The Witch Meets Dracula by Pearce Nex
Black Magic by Sue Pernatural
Witch's Coven by D. Ville Worshipper
Terrible Spells by B. Witcher
Poltergeists by Eve L. Spirit

What did Dracula ask the undertaker?
'Do you deliver?'

Why was Dracula always willing to help
 young vampires?
*Because he liked to see new blood in the
 business.*

When he was in court, what did the
   vampire promise?
*To give the tooth, the whole tooth, and
   nothing but the tooth.*

When would a vampire invite you to
   lunch?
When he fancied a bite.

Who has the most dangerous job in
   Transylvania?
Dracula's dentist.

Why was the vampire upset?
*He'd just received a letter from the manager
   of the blood bank telling him he was ten
   pints overdrawn.*

What sort of society do vampires join?
A blood group.

What frozen food company is run by
   Dracula?
Fiendus Foods.

Why was Dracula lost on the motorway?
He was looking for the main artery.

What do you get if you cross a vampire
  with a car?
*A monster that attacks vehicles and sucks
  out all their petrol.*

What is a vampire's favourite animal?
The giraffe – just think of all that neck!

Why should vampires never be trusted?
Because they are fly-by-nights.

34

How does Dracula like to eat meat?
In grave-y.

What does Count Dracula call his coffin?
His snuff-box.

Who referees the ghouls' game of cricket?
The vumpire.

How do you know that Dracula has been
    in your fruit bowl?
There are fang-marks in the blood oranges.

Why did Dracula's neighbour lend him
    £5?
Because a fiend in need is a fiend indeed.

What keeps Dracula's house guests
    awake?
His coffin.

Did you hear about the new vampire doll?
*You wind it up and it bites Barbie on the
    neck.*

What act does Dracula like best at the
    circus?
The acrobats.

What do you put on a wet vampire?
A bat robe.

What's yellow with fangs and webbed
  feet?
Count Duckula.

Why did Dracula always carry his coffin
  with him?
His life was at stake.

What do you think the tiniest vampire in
  the world gets up to at night?
Your ankles.

What do vampires gamble with?
Stake money.

What's a vampire's favourite airline?
Transylvanian Scareways.

What did Dracula give his girlfriend for
  Christmas?
A neck-lace.

What's a vampire's favourite food?
Stake and chips.

What do you get if you cross a vampire
  with Al Capone?
A fangster!

Why are Dracula's teeth like stars?
Because they come out at night.

How does a vampire enter his house?
Through the bat flap.

Why did young Dracula's mother tell him
  off?
He was fanging about with a bad set.

37

Which lady really got to Dracula's heart?
Miss Take.

Why was Dracula so happy at the races?
His horse won by a neck.

What is a vampire's favourite make of
car?
An As-tomb Martin.

What surprise did Dracula get at his office
party?
A suck-o-gram.

How do you find out if you have been
bitten by Dracula?
*Drink a glass of milk and see if your shirt
gets wet.*

What did the mummy vampire tell her
naughty son?
*'You'll get it in the neck when your father
gets home.'*

What are a vampire's favourite sweets?
Throat pastilles.

What was the vampire's favourite TV quiz
show?
The Bite is Right.

Who doesn't baby Dracula believe in?
The tooth fairy.

What would you get from a vampire that
    had lost its dentures?
A very nasty suck!

Why are vampires crazy?
Because they are often bats.

A vampire's pet bat walks into a café and orders a cup of tea. 'That'll be a pound,' said the waitress when she brought it to him. 'You know I was just thinking, we don't get many witches' bats in here . . .' 'I'm not surprised,' said the vampire's pet, 'at a pound a cup!'

Why do vampires prefer bats to cats as pets?
Because bats let themselves out at night.

Where do vampires go for their holidays?
Batlins.

Why does a vampire clean his teeth three times a day?
To prevent bat breath.

Why did the vampire's pet bat eat candles?
For light refreshment.

Was Dracula ever married?
No, he was a batchelor.

1ST BAT: Do you like Dracula films?
2ND BAT: *Yes, I think they're fangtastic!*

What is Dracula's favourite sport?
Batminton.

Where does a vampire take a bath?
In a bat tub.

2.
Weird and Wonderful Werewolves

What do you get if you cross a hairdresser
  with a werewolf?
A monster with an all-over perm.

Why shouldn't you grab a werewolf by its
  tail?
*It might be the werewolf's tail, but it could
be the end of you.*

Why are werewolves regarded as quick-
  witted?
Because they always give snappy answers.

Why did Mr and Mrs Werewolf call their
  son Camera?
Because he was always snapping.

What's the difference between a werewolf
  and a flea?
*A werewolf can have fleas but a flea can't
have werewolves.*

What do you call a hairy beast with
  clothes on?
A wear-wolf.

What do you call a hairy beast in a river?
A weir-wolf.

What do you call a hairy beast that no
  longer exists?
A were-wolf.

What do you call a hairy beast that's lost?
A where-wolf.

What happens if you cross a werewolf
  with a sheep?
You have to get a new sheep.

What do you get if you cross a werewolf
  with a flower?
*I don't know, but I wouldn't recommend
  smelling it.*

On which side does a werewolf have the
  most hair?
On the outside.

What do you get if you cross a witch with
  a werewolf?
A mad dog that chases planes.

46

'Mummy, Mummy, what's a werewolf?'
'Shut up, and comb your face.'

What is fearsome, hairy and drinks from
   the wrong side of a glass?
A werewolf with hiccups.

What happened to the wolf that fell into
   the washing-machine?
It became a wash and wear-wolf.

'I used to be a werewolf, but I'm all right nowooooooooooooo!'

How do you stop a werewolf attacking you?
Throw a stick and shout, 'Fetch!'

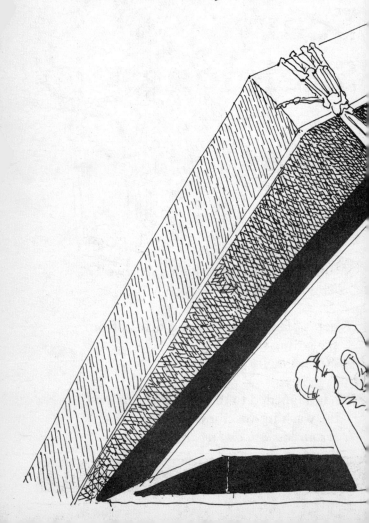

3.
Scary Skeletons

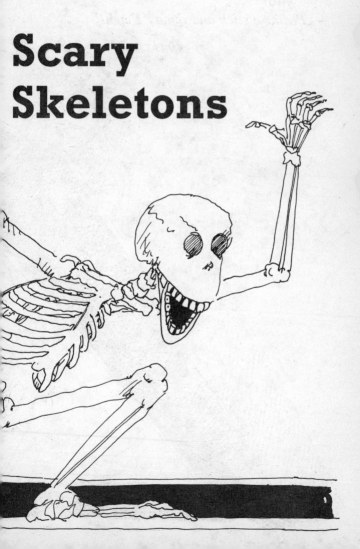

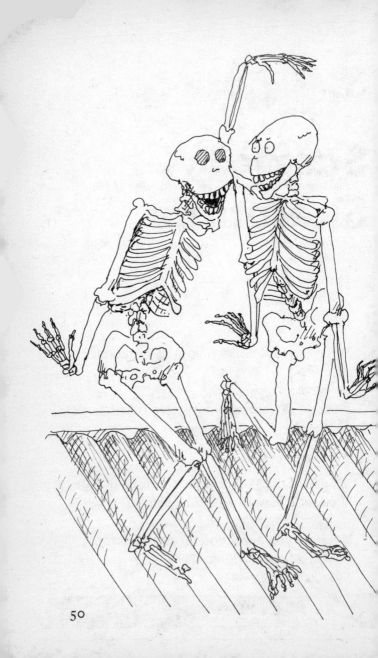

Why do skeletons hate winter?
Because the cold goes right through them.

What is the definition of noise?
Two skeletons break-dancing on a tin roof.

How do you know when a skeleton is
    upset?
He gets rattled.

What is a skeleton's favourite vegetable?
Marrow.

How do skeletons communicate with each
    other?
They use the telebone.

What did the skeleton say to his friend?
'I've got a bone to pick with you.'

What do you get if you cross a skeleton
    with a famous detective?
Sherlock Bones.

Sign in front of a cemetery: DUE TO A STRIKE, GRAVEDIGGING WILL BE DONE BY A SKELETON CREW.

What do you call a stupid skeleton?
A numbskull.

What did the old skeleton complain of?
Aching bones.

What is a skeleton?
Someone who went on a diet and forgot to say 'when'.

Did you hear about the skeleton that was attacked by a dog?
It ran off with some bones and left him without a leg to stand on.

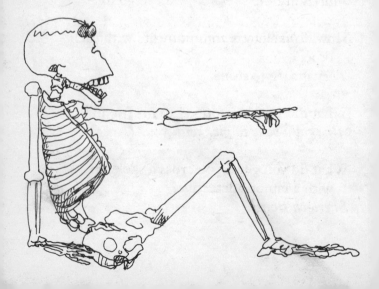

How did skeletons send each other letters
 in the days of the Wild West?
By Bony Express.

How do you make a skeleton laugh?
Easy – just tickle his funny bone.

Why are skeletons usually so calm?
Nothing gets under their skin.

What weighs a thousand kilogrammes but
 is all bone?
A skele-tonne.

What do you call a skeleton who's always
 telling lies?
A bony phony.

Why didn't the skeleton want to go to
 school?
Because his heart wasn't in it.

What's a skeleton?
Bones with the people scraped off.

Which stall did the skeletons run at the
  graveyard fête?
The rattle.

What do you call a skeleton that never
  does any work?
Lazy bones.

Why wouldn't the skeleton jump off the
  cliff?
Because he had no guts.

What is a skeleton's favourite pop group?
Boney M.

Who said 'Shiver me timbers!' on the
  ghost ship?
The skeleton crew.

Why did the skeleton go to the party?
To have a rattling good time!

What do you do if you see a skeleton
  running across the road?
Jump out of your skin and join him.

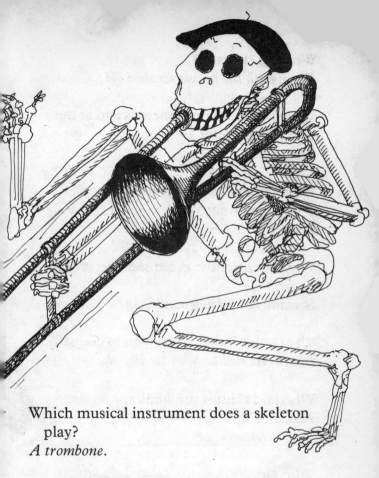

Which musical instrument does a skeleton play?
A trombone.

Which skeleton was once Emperor of France?
Napoleon Bone-apart.

What kind of plate does a skeleton eat off?
Bone china.

What did the skeleton say to his
   girlfriend?
'I love every bone in your body.'

How do ghosts pass through a locked
   door?
With a skeleton key.

What do you call a skeleton in a kilt?
Boney Prince Charlie.

Why did the one-handed skeleton cross
   the road?
To get to the second-hand shop.

Why couldn't the skeleton go to the ball?
Because he had no body to go with.

Why do skeletons drink milk?
Because it's good for the bones.

4.

Wicked Witches (Wizards too!)

What happens to a witch when she loses her temper?
She flies off the handle.

What are baby witches called?
Halloweenies.

Why do witches get good bargains?
Because they like to haggle.

What happens if you are confronted with two identical hags?
You can't tell witch is witch.

Why do wizards drink tea?
Because sorcerers need cuppas.

Why didn't the witch sing at the concert?
Because she had a frog in her throat.

What's a witch's favourite book?
Broom at the Top.

What's the witches' favourite pop group?
Broomski Beat.

Why did the witch join Tottenham
    Hotspur?
She heard they needed a new sweeper.

Why were the witches on strike?
They wanted sweeping reforms.

What do witches use pencil sharpeners
    for?
To keep their hats pointed.

What kind of jewellery do witches wear
    on their wrists?
Charm bracelets.

Why did the witch give up her job as a
    fortune-teller?
She couldn't see much future in it.

What do witches say when they overtake
    each other?
'Broom broom broom!'

What happened when the old witch went
    to see a funny film?
The manager told her to cut the cackle.

Why did the young witch have such
   difficulty writing letters?
She'd hadn't learnt to spell properly.

What do you call a wizard from outer
   space?
A flying sorcerer.

What do you call a motor bike belonging
   to a witch?
A brrooooom stick!

BROOOOOM
BROOOOOM

What do you get if you cross a sorceress
  with a millionaire?
A very witch person.

How can you tell if a witch has a glass
  eye?
When it comes out in conversation.

How do witches on broomsticks drink
  their tea?
Out of flying saucers.

What is a witch's favourite magazine?
The Witch Report!

What goes cackle, cackle, bonk?
A witch laughing her head off.

What kind of tests do they give in witch
school?
Hex-aminations.

The witches' motto:
WE CAME
WE SAW
WE CONJURED.

How can you make a witch itch?
Take away her W.

What did the doctor say to the witch?
*'Perhaps tomorrow you'll be able to get out
of bed for a spell.'*

What do you call a witch who's so nervous
she can't stop shaking?
A twitch.

Who went into the witch's den and came
out alive?
The witch.

If a flying saucer is an aircraft, does that make a broomstick a witchcraft?

What's the best way of talking to a witch?
By telephone.

WITCH IN SHOE SHOP: I'd like a pair of sandals, please.
SHOP ASSISTANT: *Certainly, madam, what kind?*
WITCH: Open-toad, of course!

Knock, knock.
Who's there?
Ivy.
Ivy who?
Ivy cast a spell on you!

1ST WITCH: I'm going to France
  tomorrow.
2ND WITCH: *Are you going by broom?*
1ST WITCH: No, by Hoovercraft.

WITCH IN PET SHOP: I've got a
  complaint. This toad you sold me keeps
  bumping into things.
PET SHOP ASSISTANT: *I expect he needs
  glasses.*
WITCH: But I can't afford to send him to
  the hoptician!

WITCH: I'd like a new frog, please.
PET SHOP ASSISTANT: *But you bought one
  only yesterday. What happened?*
WITCH: It Kermit-ted suicide.

What did the witch's cat say to the fish-
  head?
I've got a bone to pick with you.

Why do witches ride broomsticks?
*Because their vacuum-cleaner leads are too
short.*

Why does a witch ride on a broom?
A vacuum cleaner is too heavy.

What is the difference between a very
small witch and a deer that is running
from a hunter?
*One is a hunted stag, and the other is a
stunted hag.*

How does a witch tell the time?
She wears a witch watch.

1ST WITCH: Have you tried one of those new paper cauldrons?
2ND WITCH: *Yes.*
1ST WITCH: Did it work?
2ND WITCH: *No, it was tearable.*

What should you expect if you call unexpectedly on a witch at lunchtime?
Pot luck.

WITCH: I'm never coming to this restaurant again – my friend here has just swallowed a live frog!
WAITER: *Does she feel ill?*
WITCH: Ill? She'll croak at any minute!

What do you call a wicked old woman who lives by the sea?
A sandwitch.

WITCH IN SHOP: I'm looking for something to make my rock cakes light.
SHOP ASSISTANT: *I'm afraid we don't sell petrol, madam.*

What do witches like best for lunch?
Real toad-in-the-hole.

'Doctor, doctor, I think I'm a witch!'
'You'd better lie down for a spell.'

What noise does a witch's breakfast cereal make?
Snap, cackle, pop!

What is old and ugly and hangs on the line?
A drip-dry witch.

What does a witch do if her broom is stolen?
Call the Flying Squad.

What's old and ugly and goes beep beep?
A witch in a traffic jam.

Why do young witches always get As at school?
Because they're so good at spelling.

What do you call a witch who goes to the beach but won't go into the water?
A chicken sandwitch.

Did you hear about the witch who lost her bus fare?
She had to witch-hike home.

Which of the witch's friends eats the
   fastest?
The goblin.

How do witches drink tea?
With cups and sorcerers.

What kind of music do witches play on
   the piano?
Hag-time.

What happened to West Bromwitch
    Albion?
They had a spell in the First Division.

Have you heard about the weather witch?
She's forecasting sunny spells.

Two witches came out of the theatre one
    night. One said to the other, 'Shall we
    walk home, or shall we take a broom?'

What happened to the naughty witch
    schoolgirl?
She was exspelled.

Why did the witch put her broom in the
    washing-machine?
She wanted a clean sweep.

What do you call two witches who share
    a room?
Broom-mates.

5.
Mega
Monsters

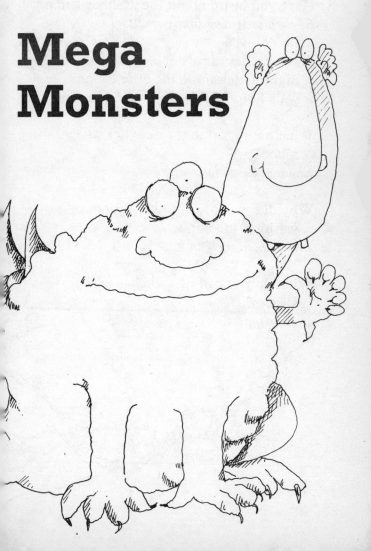

How do you raise a baby monster that has
    been abandoned by its parents?
With a fork-lift truck!

How do you keep an ugly monster in
    suspense?
I'll tell you tomorrow . . .

What eats its victims two by two?
Noah's shark.

How do you make a monster fly?
Start with a ten-foot zip.

What do you get if you cross an elephant
    with the abominable snowman?
A jumbo yeti!

Which monster has no luck?
The luckless monster.

WAITER ON OCEAN LINER: Would you like the menu, sir?

MONSTER: *No thanks, just bring me the passenger list.*

What kind of flour do short elves buy?
Elf-raising flour.

Why did Cyclops give up teaching?
He only had one pupil.

LOUISE: Your pet monster was making a terrible noise last night.

ANNA: *Yes, ever since he ate Madonna, he thinks he can sing.*

MONSTER TEACHER: If I had two people beside me, and you had two people beside you, what would we have?

MONSTER PUPIL: *Lunch!*

Why is the ghouls' football pitch wet?
Because the players keep dribbling on it.

Where is the Martian's temple?
On the side of his head.

Why did the monster lie on his back?
To trip up low-flying aircraft.

What do you get if you cross a yeti with a
  kangaroo?
A fur coat with big pockets.

Two enormous monsters fell off a cliff –
  boom boom!

What is a phantom who is married with
  seven children called?
Daddy.

What do you give a seasick monster?
Plenty of room!

How can you communicate with a ghoul
at 20,000 fathoms?
Drop him a line.

What is small, has pointed ears and is a
great detective?
Sherlock Gnomes.

What do you get if you cross a tall green
monster with a fountain pen?
The Ink-credible Hulk.

Two ghouls went duck-hunting with their
dogs, but without success.
'I know what it is, Slob,' said Grunge. 'I
know what we're doing wrong.'
'What's that then, Grunge?'
'We're not throwing the dogs high
enough!'

How can you get a set of teeth put in for
free?
Smack a monster.

Did you hear about the very well-behaved
little monster? When he was good his
father would give him ten pence and a
pat on the head. By the time he was
sixteen, he had a thousand pounds in
the bank and his head was totally flat!

What's tall, green and daft?
The Wally Green Giant.

MOTHER MUTANT: Don't eat that
   uranium.
BOY MUTANT: *Why not?*
MOTHER MUTANT: You'll get atomic-
   ache.

Ghoulish graffiti: SAY IT WITH FLOWERS
   – GIVE HER A TRIFFID.

Did you hear they now think the Loch
   Ness monster is a shark?
It's called Loch Jaws.

Where do you find wild yetis?
Depends where you leave them.

When is a bogey-man most likely to enter
   your bedroom?
When the door is open.

What do you call a monster that comes
   down your chimney at Christmas?
Santa Claws.

'How did you like the story of the
   Abominable Snowman?'
'*It left me cold.*'

What runs around Paris at lunchtime in a
   plastic bag?
The lunch-pack of Notre Dame.

Why did the mummy leave his tomb after
   4,000 years?
He felt he was old enough to leave home.

Where do you find monster snails?
On the end of monsters' fingers.

SNAIL
VARNISH

1ST GHOULISH FIEND: I had a nice man to dinner last night.
2ND GHOULISH FIEND: *So you enjoyed having him?*
1ST GHOULISH FIEND: Oh yes . . . he was delicious.

How did the midget monster get into the police force?
He lied about his height.

What did the policeman say when he met the three-headed phantom?
' 'Ello, 'ello, 'ello.'

What is the ghouls' favourite football team?
Slitherpool.

GARY GHOUL: Look, Mum, I've brought a friend home for lunch.
MOTHER GHOUL: *Good, we'll shove him in the oven.*

What did the monster do after the dentist pulled out a tooth?
He ate the dentist.

FATHER GHOUL TO DAUGHTER: You know, you really should be looking for an edible young bachelor.

Why do monsters have trouble swallowing priests and vicars?
Because it's hard to keep a good man down.

FATHER MONSTER: Johnny, don't make faces at that man. I've told you before, you mustn't play with your food.

1ST GHOUL: Am I late for dinner?
2ND GHOUL: *Yes, everyone's been eaten.*

Why are monsters so forgetful?
Because everything you tell them goes in one ear and out the others.

Why are ghouls' fingers never more than eleven inches long?
Because if they were twelve inches they'd be a foot.

What is the best thing to do if a ghoul breaks down your front door?
Run out of the back door.

MONSTER WIFE: I don't know what to make of my husband.
FRIEND: *How about a hotpot?*

What is a ghoul's favourite game?
Swallow the leader.

Did you hear about the hippie monster?
He liked to eat three squares a day.

What does a vegetarian monster eat?
Swedes.

1ST GHOUL: We had burglers last night.

2ND GHOUL: *Oh, did you?*

1ST GHOUL: Well, it made a change from slime on toast.

MR MONSTER: Oi, hurry up with my supper!

MRS MONSTER: *Oh, do be quiet – I've only got three pairs of hands.*

1ST MONSTER: The bride of Frankenstein has a lovely face.

2ND MONSTER: *If you can read between the lines.*

What did Frankenstein's monster say when he was struck by lightning?
'Great! That was just what I needed.'

Who brings the monsters their babies?
Frankenstork.

IGOR: Why is Baron Frankenstein such good fun?

MONSTER: *Because he soon has you in stitches.*

Why was Baron Frankenstein never lonely?
Because he was good at making fiends.

Did you hear what happened to
Frankenstein's monster?
*He was stopped for speeding, fined £50, and
dismantled for six months.*

How did Frankenstein's monster eat his
lunch?
He bolted it down.

What does Frankenstein's monster call a
screwdriver?
Daddy.

What is written on the grave of
    Frankenstein's monster?
Rust in Peace.

What do you call a clever monster?
Frank Einstein.

Who looks after sick gnomes?
The National Elf Service.

What do you get if you cross an Egyptian
    mummy with a car mechanic?
Toot and Car Man.

What ballet is the monster's favourite?
Swamp Lake.

MRS MONSTER TO MR MONSTER: 'Try to
    be nice to my mother when she visits
    us this weekend, dear. Fall down when
    she hits you!'

6.
Ghostly
Ghosts

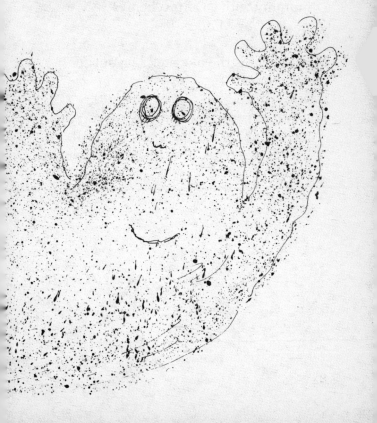

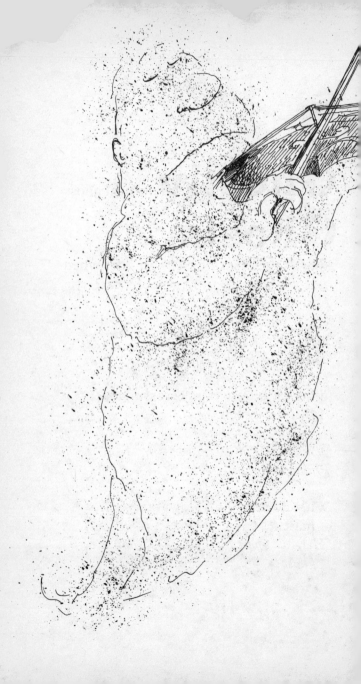

What sort of violin does a musical ghost
  play?
A dreadivarius.

What's the first thing a ghost does when
  it gets into the front seat of a car?
Fasten the sheet belt.

How do ghosts learn songs?
They read the sheet music.

Where do ghost-trains cross roads?
At devil crossings.

Which weight do ghosts box at?
Phantom weight.

What do phantoms sing at football
  matches?
*'Here we ghost, here we ghost, here we
  ghost . . .'*

Which ghost was President of France?
Charles de Ghoul.

What do you get if you cross a ghost with
a packet of crisps?
Snacks that go crunch in the night.

What does a ghost call its parents?
Mum and Dead.

What do ghosts eat?
Dread and Butter pudding.

How do ghosts like their eggs?
Terror-fried!

Did you hear about the famous ghost politician?
He became Spooker of the House of Commons.

Why are old ghosts boring?
Because they're groan-ups.

What did one hippie ghost say to the other hippie ghost?
'Real ghoul, man.'

Where do ghosts live?
In dread-sitters.

What is a ghost's favourite book?
Ghoul-liver's Travels.

How do English ghosts go abroad?
By British Scareways.

What did the ghost call his mother and father?
His transparents.

How can you tell if a ghost is about to faint?
It goes as white as a sheet.

1ST BOY: I met a ghost last night.
2ND BOY: *What did it say?*
1ST BOY: I don't know – I can't speak dead languages.

What do you call a TV show that stars ghosts and phantoms?
A spook-tacular.

What did the teacher ghost say to the lazy pupil ghosts?
'You don't seem to have any school spirit any more!'

Why are cemeteries so popular?
Who knows, but people are dying to get into them!

Why did the ghost go into hospital?
To have his ghoul-stones removed.

Where do ghosts send their laundry?
To the dry screamers.

What phantom was a famous painter?
Vincent Van Ghost.

If you tipped a can of food over a ghoul,
   what would you get?
Beans on ghost.

Why did the ghosts hold a seance?
To try to contact the living.

At the ghosts' school, what song is sung
   each morning?
Ghoul Britannia.

1ST GHOST: I've just bought a haunted bicycle.
2ND GHOST: *How do you know it's haunted?*
1ST GHOST: There are spooks in the wheels.

Why did the ghost look in the mirror?
To make sure he still wasn't there!

What country has the most ghosts?
Ghosta Rica.

What do you call it when a ghost makes a mistake?
A boo-boo.

What is a ghost's favourite day of the week?
Moanday.

What do you call ghost children?
Boys and ghouls.

What did one ghost say to the other?
'It's nice not to see you again.'

How do ghosts begin a letter?
'Tomb it may concern . . .'

Who appears on the front of horror
   magazines?
The cover ghoul!

What do baby ghosts like chewing?
Boo-ble gum.

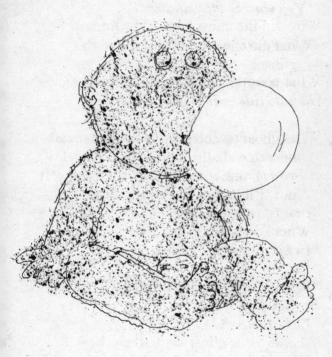

What is the ghost's favourite Wild West
town?
Tombstone.

What's a ghost's favourite fairground
   ride?
The Roller Ghoster.

What did the little boy say when he saw
   the ghost of Charles I?
'You must be off your head!'

What did the estate agent say to the
   ghost?
*'I'm sorry, sir, we have nothing suitable for
   haunting at the moment.'*

The ghost teacher was showing her class
   how to walk through walls. 'Now did
   you all understand that?' she asked. 'If
   not, I'll just go through it again . . .'

Where do space ghosts live?
In far distant terror-tory.

Which is the ghost's favourite stretch of
   water?
Lake Eerie.

Did you hear about Romeo Ghost meeting
   Juliet Ghost?
It was love at first fright.

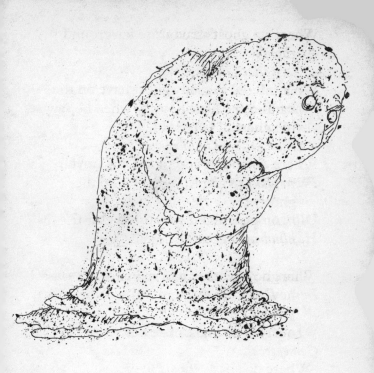

Why did the ghost's shroud fall down?
Because he had no visible means of support!

Why are ghosts always poor?
*Because a ghoul and his money are soon
  parted.*

What is big, invisible, has four wheels and
  flies?
The Ghost Town dustcart.

Where do ghosts study?
At ghoul-lege.

What job did the lady ghost have on the jumbo jet?
Air Ghostess.

Where do ghouls and phantoms travel?
From ghost to ghost.

Did you hear about the stupid ghost?
He climbed over walls.

Where do ghosts like to swim?
In the Dead Sea.

What trees do ghosts like best?
Ceme-trees.

What is the best way for a ghost hunter to keep fit?
Exorcise regularly.

What is a ghost's favourite music?
Haunting melodies.

What do you call twin ghosts who keep ringing doorbells?
Dead ringers.

What game do ghosts like to play at
  parties?
Haunt and seek.

1ST GHOST: I find haunting castles really
  boring these days.
2ND GHOST: *I know what you mean. I
  just don't seem able to put any life into
  it.*

Who puts the ghosts' point of view at
  their press conference?
A spooksman.

What do ghosts buy to put in their
  coffee?
Evaporated milk.

What do you do with a green ghost?
Wait until he's ripe.

Why do demons and ghouls get on so
  well?
Because demons are a ghoul's best friend.

Which ghost made friends with the three
  bears?
Ghouldilocks.

Where do ghosts stay when they go on
  holiday?
At a ghost-house.

1ST GHOST: I don't seem to frighten
  people any more.
2ND GHOST: *I know. We might as well be
  dead for all they care.*

Why is the graveyard such a noisy place?
Because of all the coffin!

What kind of horse would a headless
   horseman ride?
A nightmare.

What jewels do ghosts wear?
Tombstones.

What is a ghost's final drink?
His bier.

What do you get if you cross a ghost with
   a potato?
A spook-tater.

Where would a Red Indian's ghost live?
In a creepy tepee.

What do ghostly soldiers say to strangers?
'*Who ghost there?*'

1ST GHOST: You give me eerie ache!
2ND GHOST: *Sorry I spook.*

What do ghosts like about riding horses?
Ghoulloping.

Why are ghosts invisible?
They wear see-through clothes.

What is the name of the ghost's favourite
     pub?
The Horse and Gloom.

Why did the ghost teacher tell off the
     ghost pupil?
Because he kept making a ghoul of himself.

What would you do if you found that your
     bedroom was haunted?
Find another bedroom.

What do you get if you cross a ghost with
   a boy scout?
*A ghost that scares old ladies across the
   street.*

What is a ghost's favourite dessert?
Boo-berry pie with I-scream.

MOTHER GHOST TO SON: How many
   times do I have to tell you – spook when
   you are spooken to.

1ST GHOST: I saw *The Phantom of the
   Opera* on television last night.
2ND GHOST: *Was it frightening?*
1ST GHOST: Yes, it half scared the life
   into me!

What do you call a ghost doctor?
A surgical spirit.

How do worried ghosts look?
Grave.

How do ghosts keep their feet dry?
By wearing boo-ts.

What do you call a ghost that has had too
   much to drink at a party?
A methylated spirit.

How do ghosts like their drinks in
summer?
Ice ghoul.

Where are the ghosts when the lights go
out?
In the dark.

Why are ghosts bad at telling lies?
Because you can see right through them.

What did one ghost say to another?
*'I'm sorry, but I just don't believe in
people.'*

What do ghosts call their navy?
The Ghost Guard.

What do you flatten a ghost with?
A spirit level.

What did the barman say when the ghost
ordered a gin and tonic?
'Sorry, we don't serve spirits.'

Which ghost has the best hearing?
The eeriest.

Why did the lady marry a ghost?
She didn't know what possessed her.

What do ghosts eat for supper?
Spook-etti.

What do short-sighted ghosts wear?
Spook-tacles.

What walks through walls saying 'Boo'
very quietly?
A nervous ghost.

What trembles and says 'Oob'?
A nervous ghost walking through a wall backwards.

What do you call a play that's acted by ghosts?
A phantomime.

What do ghosts eat for breakfast?
Dreaded wheat.

What do ghosts eat for lunch?
Ghoul-ash.

What position does a ghost play in a football team?
Ghoulie.

THE GREAT PUFFIN JOKE DIRECTORY
Brough Girling

Over 1,000 jokes presented alphabetically with Fat Puffin to guide you through. An original, hilarious book – you'll never be short of a laugh again!

CHUCKLE, CHUCKLE, THE CHILDREN'S JOKE BOOK
Ann Leadercramer and Rosalind Morris

An original and entertaining collection of jokes, puzzles and riddles from St Anthony's School, Hampstead, in aid of the Wishing Well Appeal.

UP WITH SKOOL!

A book of jokes from children themselves, divided into ten sections including school dinners, homework and exams, and introduced by Mr Majeika.

THE SECOND PUFFIN CROSSWORD PUZZLE BOOK

Alan Cash

Another challenging crossword puzzle collection, including specialist puzzles for experts in science, literature and loads of other subjects. There are plenty of cryptic and general clues, too – enough to keep all crossword addicts happy.

ENVIRONMENTALLY YOURS

Early Times

What is the greenhouse effect? Why is the Earth getting warmer? Who is responsible for the destruction of the countryside? Where can you get advice on recycling? When will the Earth's resources run out? The answers to all these questions and many more are given in this forthright and informative book. Topics such as transport, industry, agriculture, population and energy are covered as well as lists of 'green' organizations and useful addresses.

THE HA-HA BONK BOOK

Janet and Allan Ahlberg

This joke book is full of old jokes to tell dads, mums, baby brothers, teachers and just about anybody else you can think of!

THE D-I-Y GENIUS KIT
Gyles Brandreth

An hilarious guide on how to gain the entire world know-ledge – all in one box! With amazing facts at your fingertips you can stun your friends – and we guarantee that absolutely no mental equipment is necessary!

THE CHRISTMAS STOCKING JOKE BOOK
Shoo Rayner

A joke book that every child will enjoy, packed with lots of festive jokes and cartoons.

RUDOLPH'S CHRISTMAS FUN BOOK
Martyn Forrester

Sacks full of Christmas crosswords, Christmas quizzes, Christmas facts, Christmas puzzles PLUS games, tricks, jokes, codes and lots more fun things to do. Beats watching the Christmas edition of your favourite soap any day! This one will sleigh you, as Rudolph says.

CROSSWORD CRACKERS
Colin Gumbrell

A carefully thought out, original, and inventive collection of crosswords with clues covering a wide range of general knowledge.

MORE CROSSWORD CRACKERS
Colin Gumbrell

Nuts may be easier to crack than these crosswords, but they aren't half the fun! Three different sorts of crosswords ensure there's never a dull moment with the puzzles in this fascinating and original book. Whether you're a beginner or an experienced puzzler, you can be certain that there will be plenty to intrigue and delight you.

PUZZLER'S A to Z
Colin Gumbrell

Puzzle your way from A to Z with these inventive and entertaining anagrams, word searches, shape and number puzzles, crosswords and quizzes of all kinds.